Karl
the Grateful Dog

Karl
the Grateful Dog

A story of rescue...

By

Jeff Ousley and Penny Wagner

Illustrated by Chris Ousley

Karl the Grateful Dog
Copyright © 2014 by Jeff Ousley and Penny Wagner. All rights reserved.
First published by Strategic Book Publishing & Rights Agency, LLC (August 5, 2014)
Stonewall Press Edition published 2018

No part of this publication may be reproduced, stored in a retrieval system or transmitted in any way by any means, electronic, mechanical, photocopy, recording or otherwise without the prior permission of the author except as provided by USA copyright law.

The opinions expressed by the author are not necessarily those of Stonewall Press.

Published in the United States of America

ISBN: 978-1-64460-037-5 (*sc*)
      978-1-64460-036-8 (*e*)

Library of Congress Control Number: 2018961898

Book Design/Layout by Kalpart. Visit www.kalpart.com
Cover photo by Jeff Ousley

Stonewall Press books may be ordered through booksellers or by contacting:

Stonewall Press
4800 Hampden Lane, Suite 200
Bethesda, MD 20814 USA
www.stonewallpress.com
1-888-334-0980
orders@stonewallpress.com

1. Family
2. Pets
14 November 2018 5:49 AM

"He loved deeply and tried dogfully."

John Steinbeck

Table of Contents

Penny's Post — 8

Prologue
Kismet — 10

Chapter One
The Meeting — 12

Chapter Two
The Decision — 23

Chapter Three
Are We Going Home? — 31

Chapter Four
The Garden — 38

Chapter Five
The Sunset — 43

Chapter Six
Finally Home — 49

Jeff's Note — 55

Penny's Post

It is hard to explain or understand indeterminate events in our life. Isn't it? When I met Karl, my best friend was a slobbery tongue boy/dog named Kingsley. My kids grown away, he was my family. Together, King and I would walk the beach and life was a 'Love Life' sojourn. It seemed that trumpets awakened us to the coming day's sunrise, summer was always day, and night eased in a sheepish serenity. It was all…

It was soon to be, I was given a half chance, a kind of poor share, of a second marvelous mutt, a yellow dog of a serious and silly nature. He was too grand, for even his grand size, a man sized king/dog ready and wanting to be grander as he 'wiggle butted' perfectly along the margins of life, tail toasting away worry and loneliness. Every moment to be with Karl is to have Karl be *in you*.

Jeff's dog knowhow, Karl's bowing to something else that he knows that is better than us, has created the ultimate service dog. Rescuing sick children, gals and guys from kiddie schools to nursing homes, he's blind to differences and is never indifferent. When he's home, with Jeff, he becomes a kind of rockstar boy scout, ready to slam jam and then roll home with Jeff a 1 and 2 perfect timing tied in together to two kind, kind souls. It is said that a dog will actually change his heartbeat to match the one he loves. I believe Karl may have three heartbeats, Jeff's, mine and God's.

Book two will be dedicated to Karl but when he gets his real voice, he is loved that much, he'll dedicate a book to Jeff who saved him and to me who helped.

Peace Be With You,
Penny

Prologue

Kismet

"Love is our true destiny. We do not find the meaning of life by ourselves alone—we find it with another."

Thomas Merton

One spring morning, I received an email from the local SAFE shelter asking me to provide transportation and an emergency foster home for a dog named Carl. I expected to read the details, and off I'd go. But something was different and a little awkward. All the messages and pictures I've received from them before had to be downloaded to view. This time, the picture of a lanky yellow lab instantly filled my phone screen. I remember sitting down staring quietly at his picture.

The SAFE shelter that contacted me operated a thrift store. I went there to receive the paperwork. One customer purchased a piece of furniture at the store. He was struggling as he tried to place this large piece of furniture in his not-so-large car. Since I was driving my truck, I loaded the piece onboard for him and took it to his home.

"Take this twenty dollars for helping," he said. I refused the money, but he insisted. I was left with no choice and began the journey to pick up Carl with two ten-dollar bills tucked in my pocket.

I knew I could use the money to buy a leash and collar for the huge dog that bedazzled me from the beginning, whom I would rename Karl with a "K". I fell in love on that beautiful May day. My name is Jeff and Karl is my dog. *Karl the Grateful Dog* is our story.

Chapter One

The Meeting

A man and his loneliness often live together in silence.

"Ruff," Carl wanted to say as he looked out from the wire cage. "Ruff."

But no voice came out. Too many people had passed and no one had stopped to open the metal door.

"Ruff," was what he *really* wanted to say. Instead, Carl stared in silence.

Carl placed his chin on the hard floor. His gentle amber eyes turned to the sound of a door being opened. One ear was cocked to listen. He heard talking.

"I'm here to pick up the yellow lab and bring him to a SAFE

shelter," said a man with a pleasant smile. He showed a picture of a dog to the glitzy woman who worked in the shelter's office. The woman's name was Gloria.

Thump, thump, thump. Carl's yellow tail slowly knocked on the cage floor. He knew he must be the dog in the picture.

"Yes, Carl is here," answered Gloria. She reached through the mesh and poked the lanky lab near his drooping mouth. "He's too big. Nobody wants him."

The man stood in front of Carl's cage. He looked down at Carl.

"And," said Gloria, "he doesn't bark."

Carl sat up. He tucked his tail under him. He wanted to go with the man, but he was afraid.

Gloria grabbed the gate's latch and opened the enclosure. The metal door screeched across the rough surface of the cement.

Carl anxiously backed away as Gloria reached in to snatch his collar. He felt his hear jump in his chest. He turned around and his collar twisted. Gloria lost her grip.

Carl saw the grimace on Gloria's face, and he wasn't sure if she would push the door closed again. He didn't want to sleep in a shelter anymore. He wanted a home.

The man who had been watching him seemed to understand. "Carl, come on," he said quietly. "Carl, come on."

Carl was confused. He stared at the open door.

As Gloria turned to talk to the man, Carl darted from the cage.

"Carl," screamed Gloria, "stop!"

Something from Carl's past urged him to keep going. *Run, run, run!*

Carl couldn't read or he would have run to the door marked *Exit*. Instead, he ran down the walkway and came to a sudden stop. He was stuck between several stacked cages and a large lavender door. In the center of the bright colored door were the words *Keep Out*. There was nowhere to go. Carl was trapped.

"Carl," Gloria screamed, "*stay*."

Run, run, run! thought Carl. He was scared.

As the cages fell to the cement floor, several of the doors were flung open. Now, a spotted hound named Buddy and a brown dog named Larry ran behind Carl. A cat named Mercedes was able to hide behind some nearby boxes.

Gloria dashed through the narrow aisle and managed to grab Buddy. Larry sat down at her angry order, "Stay!"

Mercedes ventured back to her toppled cage. Carl continued to run looking for a way to escape.

At last, Carl leaped at the large lavender door. He fell against the metal handle. The door flew open and he crashed to the floor with a titanic *thud*. A step ladder plummeted down and knocked over several jugs of bubbly cleaning fluid.

An oversized broom toppled over, missing Carl but knocking Gloria right on top of her head. "Ugh!" she cried.

Still trying to catch Carl, she lunged forward to grab him by his tail, but instead clutched the handle of an enormous floor mop. Slipping on the soupy, soapy suds that covered the floor, she landed squarely on her back. "Oomph!" was the peculiar sound which burst from her mouth as the mop flopped over her eyes.

Leaning back against the closet's whitewashed wall, Gloria gasped for breath. But, on a narrow shelf above her head was a half-empty can of gooey orange gunk. The pandemonium had knocked the right shelf bracket free, and the can came skating off the edge.

The spinning can missed Gloria, but as it hit the floor it exploded, and dribbles of gooey orange glop flew up and covered Gloria. Determined to help, the man tossed to her the first thing he could find – the shelter manager's white coat. Gloria began to dab the sticky orange splotches from her face.

"You crazy dog," Gloria mumbled. Then she realized the orange mess was all over the manager's white coat and she shrieked. She looked up at the man who now wore a muddled grin and she said, "Get that dog out of here right now, and you get out of here, too." She tossed two crumpled papers at him as he began to turn away.

Carl knew he had to find a way out of the shelter.

Suddenly the man stepped into Carl's view. "Come, Carl," he said in a gentle voice. "Come."

Carl stopped and stared. The man eased closer.

"Carl, come with me," said the man in a reassuring voice. Soft and soothing. "Come, Carl, come. Everything will be all right. Come."

Carl leaned back. The man looked at the huge dog who had propped himself awkwardly against the shelter's bare wall. His front legs began to slide forward. The man leaned over him and Carl lifted his large yellow paw into the air.

Reaching for Carl, the man took the paw and shook it up and down. He said, "Carl, my name is Jeff."

Jeff quietly fastened a leash on Carl's collar, and they quickly left the shelter. As Jeff opened the driver's door of his silver truck, Carl hurtled past him. His huge puppy-like body became hung up on the console. His liver-colored nose slammed into the volume knob on the stereo as his front legs shuffled in the air. Despite his uncomfortable landing, Carl still kept silent. After moving himself to the passenger's side, he bowed his head in what could almost be seen as a gesture of gratitude. Carl turned to look at Jeff.

As Jeff drove his truck down the bumpy streets, Carl sat looking through the windows. His large front paws were braced against the floorboards while his oversized body sat comfortably on the padded seat. When Carl had whacked the radio knob, the volume had been forced up and the stereo screamed out. But Jeff did not turn it down. Carl and Jeff's heads bounced together in rhythm with the solid rock and roll sounds coming from the truck's speakers.

Still, Carl did not bark.

Chapter Two

The Decision

Your heart will not betray you.

Dawdling down the highway, Jeff spotted a crooked sign that read *BBQ Sandwiches*. It pointed to a worn-out yellow trailer. A red neon light blinked, "Open! Open! Open! Open!" The trailer's rusty roof had a rounded shape, and sticking out from it was a tattered tan tarp covering a lopsided picnic table. The left rear tire of the trailer was flat and the unit stooped lower on that side. Even with the trailer's shabby look, the sweet smell of tangy BBQ pork drew the two travelers in.

"Carl, do you want to share a sandwich?"

Carle's pinkish-purple tongue twirled slowly from side to side. *Mmmmmmmmmm*, he thought.

Jeff and Carl walked to the window of the trailer and bought a sandwich from the angry-looking BBQ man whose polo shirt said *Otto*.

Then Jeff dropped the tailgate on the silver truck and he and Carl sat down. Jeff took a big bite of the sweet saucy sandwich, but Carl finished his half with an enormous *chomp*.

"Carl, did you even taste that sandwich?" Jeff asked with a light laugh. That's when he noticed that the fur on Carl's lower back was thin and bare. Spotty red rashes highlighted the hurts.

"Carl, what happened?" asked Jeff sadly, as he gently stroked Carl's broad crown.

"Ruff," was what Carl wanted to say.

Jeff gave Carl a huge hug and looked deep into his downcast doggie eyes. He saw something inside those eyes that told him of Carl's sad past. But then Carl's eyes grew bigger. His chin moved higher and he stared back deep into Jeff's eyes. Carl saw worry and work and he knew Jeff needed him, too. He wished he could use real words and say, "Jeff, I'll be your dog."

Suddenly, both heads squared and they looked straight at each other. Then Jeff straightened the papers that Gloria had tossed at him. He read aloud, "Carl-yellow lab-deliver to a SAFE shelter in St. Augustine."

Carl heard the word *shelter*.

Run, run, run!

Carl jumped off the tailgate of the truck. His unsteady landing forced his two front paws to buckle and his nose punched the ground. He pulled himself up, preparing to run again.

Beside the crooked picnic table was a cranky calico cat. The corner of Carl's eye caught the sight of the feisty furball and, momentarily distracted, he plunged at the crabby kitty. The cat's claws swiped the side of Carl's sore nose. He retreated just long enough for the cat to skitter away, and then he began the chase again. They sprinted under the table, onto the bench, to the top of the table, scuttling up and down, cat and Carl, Carl and cat, under and on top, again and again.

"Get your mutt away from my Dottie Sue!" hollered Otto.

"Come, Carl, come. You can't chase that cat," Jeff pleaded. He jumped from the tailgate of the truck in panicked pursuit of his four-legged fugitive.

Otto ordered, "Out! Out! Get that mutt out of here!"

Dottie Sue dodged under the dilapidated trailer. Carl charged after the faster feline. His front right shoulder shoved into the metal pole which held up the tattered tarp. It fell over, covering Jeff who had just jogged over to try to stop him. Twisting and turning, Jeff tried to tear himself free from the heavy tarp. Finally, Otto, more ornery than ever, plucked the pair from under the tarp.

"I said, get that dog out of here—and you get out of here, too," Otto shouted.

Jeff's hand held tight to Carl's collar. "Carl! Stay with me!" he said sternly as Carl stubbornly tried to yank away. All Carl wanted to do was run.

Luckily, Jeff was able to secure the leash, and Carl was forced to give in to Jeff's command. Dottie Sue chose to retreat up a tree. She looked down triumphantly, her tail swishing and her fur spiked all down her back.

Carl looked up at the cross kitty. He wanted to bark at her, but still he was silent.

Jeff apologized to Otto and offered him two ten-dollar bills to help to pay for the tarp. Otto snatched the money and screamed, "*Go!*"

Jeff opened the truck door and nodded to Carl to jump inside. This time, Carl politely pushed in past Jeff.

"Carl, what happened? Who hurt you? Why do you want to run away?"

Carl's soft, silky ears tucked tight to the sides of his huge head. His downtrodden doggie look told a tale of loneliness and a lack of love.

"Carl, do you want to come home with me? Do you want to be my dog?" asked Jeff.

Carl turned around two times on the truck's padded passenger seat and laid his chin securely on Jeff's right hand. Jeff eased the shift knob from park to drive, moving the position carefully so he wouldn't disturb Carl's rest.

Jeff looked tenderly towards the oversized puppy with his red scars. Tears dropped from his chin and landed on top of Carl's broad head. "You're my boy. From now on, you'll be Carl, but it will be Karl with a *K*."

Karl looked up, his tongue dropping slightly from his mouth, and smiled. He nodded his head up and down, up and down, as if to say, "Yes, yes!" His sad amber eyes brightened and his tail moved thunderously from side to side. Karl was a grateful dog.

Chapter Three

Are We Going Home?

"Life brings us to unexpected places—love brings us home."

Jeff and Karl continued rambling down the road with the stereo roaring with the sounds of "Ramble On Rose," recorded from an early eighties classic rock show. Karl loved the music. With one amber eye closed and one partly opened, his head bobbed high and low, bouncing with the beat and marvelously matching the music's melody.

"Did you say your name was Ramblin' Rose?

Ramble on baby, settle down easy

Ramble on Rose…"

Jerry Garcia, Robert Hunter

But Karl still did not bark.

Jeff turned down a narrow side street making a right, left, left, right and right turn. His truck skidded to a stop in his driveway. Large and small chips of loose gravel spun out from under the chrome chassis.

"Karl, we're home!" Jeff said with a soft smile.

Karl stood up to look out the front window. His front paws were, again, straight on the floorboard while his whole hind end wiggled and his back legs, propped awkwardly on the seat, wobbled as he tried to see his new home.

But, at the second, something inside Karl changed. His oversized tail dragged between his legs. Something from his past urged him to go. *Run, run, run* was all he could think of doing. With his nose pressed against the car door, Karl was ready for this final escape. Jeff moved around and opened the passenger door and Karl leaped from the seat. His huge haunch hit Jeff and pushed him aside.

But his time, Jeff was able to grab Karl. He nudged the nervous dog toward the front entrance of his home. Hurriedly unlocking the front door, Jeff guided Karl inside. Karl's chin drooped. He clumsily sank to the floor, too afraid even to look around or up at Jeff. Jeff knew how Karl was feeling. He crossed the room to do what he always did when he felt this same way. He turned the music on.

"Karl, you're all right. We're home!" said Jeff.

Karl didn't want to listen to the music. He sadly rolled his eyes away and whined over the sounds coming from the stereo. Instinctively, Jeff jerked the stereo knob up and Neil Young exploded from the speakers. "Karl, this is Mr. Young singing 'Mansion on the Hill'"

Karl lifted himself from the floor and wearily walked away from where he and Jeff had been. He looked longingly at the door, wishing Jeff would open it. He wanted to run down the road.

"There's a mansion on the hill..." Karl heard these words and looked at Jeff. The magic of rock suddenly seemed to roll through Karl and the tangle of words and music touched him in a tender way.

"Music fills the air." Jeff and Karl continued to listen to the tune together.

Karl collapsed again, but this time he moved closer to the console that carried the carousel of songs.

"Peace and love live there still." *Peace and love*, though Karl.

Jeff and Karl nodded as the notes came streaming through the stereo. Karl's thunderous tail began to swish in sync with the song.

"In that mansion on the hill." Jeff pumped Karl's paws up and down in pattern with the notes. Karl's head moved with the music and his powerful paws continued to punch lightly at the floor, keeping the rhythm right. At the same time, his amber eyes rolled around the room. He paused to focus on many of the framed posters of framed rock greats. A gaggle of guitars was given some space in the corner of the giant room.

"Karl, you're going to be happy here," said Jeff.

Suddenly the music changed, and Jeff tipped his head toward the stereo. "Karl this is Heart, my big sisters of rock, singing 'Dog and Butterfly.'" Jeff lightly lifted Karl's ear and sang the lyrics, "With a little tear in her eye, she had to try, she had to try—Dog and Butterfly."

Karl picked himself up from the floor and moved right under the speakers.

Jeff could tell that Karl understood the magic message of music.

A dog will know when the song is right, thought Jeff, remembering those worthwhile words by Mr. Shakey, the iconic music man, and *you just proved it."*

As the music filled the house, it poured through into the backyard.

Chapter Four

The Garden

"Gardens are a form of autobiography."

Sydney Eddison

"Karl, let's go see what's outside," said Jeff.

Jeff and Karl vaulted down the back steps. They collided into a kaleidoscope of colorful flowers and vegetables. There were collard greens, red and yellow peppers, a peach tree and a pomegranate bush, along with bouquets of purple basil. This teddy bear of a dog was touched by the display of tender plants. He walked beside Jeff weaving along on the patchwork pattern of pavers.

Karl gazed at the guitar-shaped garden gloriously growing oranges and other fancy fruits. In the center of this peaceful place was a hammock that hung horizontally between two brown boards. Jeff jumped into this cozy cradle.

"Karl, it's time to take a nap," said Jeff. "Don't you need a nap, too?"

Karl jumped into the hammock with Jeff. On the ground beneath them was a Caffe Vita burlap coffee bag. Jeff had placed it there to kneel on as he pulled the weeds that were working their way through a bed of yellow and red butterfly bushes.

If you have a mind at peace,

A heart that cannot harden.

Go find a door that opens wide,

Upon a lovely garden.

As they both dozed off, Karl's doggie dream drew him into a delightful daze of days in his happy musical home, as he envisioned helping his Jeff build a very big vegetable garden.

Jeff smiled. He dreamed about Karl liking long road trips, wiping away work worries, helping to build garden beds, and making music matter most. These backyard buddies slept soundly, but there was something that had been seen only by Karl. The garden gate was left unlatched.

The afternoon sun came streaming through the partition of green limbs that formed an umbrella over the pair. Jeff moved from the hammock and began to harrow the rich garden soil. Sunshine stoked Karl. He moved from the hammock to lie down on the burlap coffee bag. Soon he moved again to lounge lazily on an oversized blue chair. He was close to the unfastened fence. He wished this could work and that he could live forever with wonderful Jeff. But nothing had ever worked out for him.

Karl's steady stare continued circling the grounds. He noticed two sassy squirrels that scurried under the fence, but he did not chase them.

"Karl, we're almost done now," said Jeff as he moved towards the gate.

Karl really did like Jeff. He liked the gardens. He liked the music, but this wasn't enough to make him stay. Lack of trust began to tear through him. Too much discipline and doggie don'ts from this distant days had damaged his developing devotion to Jeff. He suddenly dove from the big blue chair and careened toward the unfastened fence. He tore through the unguarded gate and ran towards trouble.

Chapter Five

The Sunset

"Every sunset brings the promise of a new dawn."

Ralph Waldo Emerson

Run, run, run across the paved street, through an empty lot, towards the busy road. Karl was confused. He remembered loneliness, a chain, being tied to a fence, no friends, rain, rocks, hunger, hurts.

Karl scampered through the first lane of traffic. A small buggy-like car nearly hit him and a rider on a bicycle had to dash up the curb to avoid the fast-moving yellow lab. A flashing school bus tooted its horn. *Beep!*

But Karl ran on with Jeff in pursuit. Jeff shouted, "Karl, come back! Karl, come back!" But Karl charged across to the opposite side of the street.

A small boy named Michael was leaving the last step of the bus when Karl and Jeff ran by. He dropped his school bag and began to run after the runaways. "Hey, come back! Doggie, stop! Come back!" screamed Michael as he dashed after Karl and Jeff.

Run, run, run was all that was on Karl's mind.

The boy's big brother, who had been waiting for Michael at the bus stop, joined the chase. "Hey, Michael, come back," bellowed the big brother. "Come back."

A passerby who was walking down the street with several bags of groceries was spun around as Karl, Jeff, the boy and now, the big brother ran by. The passerby dropped his bags on the hard pavement, splitting a carton of eggs. The eggs cracked open and spilled on the sidewalk. Leaving the mess, he decided to chase the yellow rascal, too.

"Hey, come back! Somebody's gotta pay for this!" the irate man shouted. "Come back!"

It was beginning to get dark. Shades of pink highlighted the sky as the sun sank into the horizon. Magenta colors reflected everywhere along Karl's route. As Karl paced himself, a pink hue cast a circular shadow all around him, and above his broad crown it looked like the wispy image of an angel's halo. His long legs loped in perfect rhythm with the rock and roll sound from the surfside scene just ahead. Karl's giant tail swung in sync with the beat. He deliberately paused for a minute, listening to the positive sound of the music, thinking about Jeff and their ride home together. He had good memories of the merry melodies on the truck's stereo. The bedazzled dog dashed on. He ran happily towards the familiar bouncy beat and into the huge crowd of music-lovers.

Karl darted around a man selling ice cream from a cart. As he cruised by, he accidentally knocked into a lady who had stopped to buy some cold treats for her three small children.

"Puppy, puppy, puppy," chanted the children and they buoyantly began to chase after Karl, too.

As the mother jerked forward to foil the boys' fun, she slipped and accidentally slapped strawberry ice cream across the red-and-white striped shirt of another boy name Billy.

"Sorry, I didn't mean it. That mutt's a menace, "said the mom as she began to run after her trio.

Billy screamed, "My shirt is all sticky!" and he jumped in to join the train-like parade charging after Karl. Running with Billy was Jeff,

the boy named Michael, his big brother, the irate man, the mother with three small boys, and now, a police officer. All of them shouting in unison, "Hey, come back! Come Back!"

"Stop that darn dog!" the police officer said, and then he blasted a note on his whistle.

Karl ran up the steps of the pavilion toward the rock and roll coming from the stage. Still moving forward, he zigzagged around several dancing couples. The loud music and the noisy crowd chasing him began to frighten him. He tried to stop himself. His powerful paws reached forward and pushed hard against the dance floor. He skidded sideways. He tried frantically to prevent himself from colliding with a guitarist. Instead, his thick tail caught the drummer's stand and the cymbals crashed onto the cement floor. Luckily, the guitar player was able to jump over the massive moving puppy. Karl's liver-colored nose whacked into the back of the stage and he came to a forceful sudden stop.

The other band members stopped playing the crowd stepped

back. Waves of *Oooooohhhhs* and *Aaaaahhhhhs* flowed through the crowd.

Still, Karl did not bark.

Chapter Six

Finally Home

Home isn't a place—it's having companionship; someone who loves you. Karl and I are now home.

Karl lay with his chin on the concrete floor. He was hurt, hungry, and humiliated. Then something from his not-so-distant past caused him to pick up his head. His left ear lifted to listen.

"Karl, where are you? Karl, come home," said a familiar, friendly voice. Karl remembered his freedom, his first friend, the silver truck, the BBQ sandwich, real music, Karl with a *K*, and a new home.

Michael, the big brother, the irate man, the mom, three small boys, and the police officer burst into the melee. They were all tense and tired, and tears of exhaustion rolled down the littlest children's cheeks.

"I found him! He's right here!" said the little boy, Michael, and he hugged the dazed and dizzy dog.

Karl's soft amber eyes looked lovingly back at the little boy.

Michael's big brother made him move away from the dog. "Hope you'll find a happy home," said the bigger boy.

The irate man looked at the immense tail on the big yellow dog as it slowly went *thump, thump—thump, thump*.

"This dog didn't do anything wrong," said the man, no longer irate. "Why, anyone can see he's just scared. Why wouldn't he be? Just let him go."

"My puppy, my puppy, *my* puppy, *mine*!" The three little boys begged to take Karl home. "Please can we take him home? We can buy him a toy."

"You're too young. Guess who would end up taking care of him?" said the mother as she shook her head. "Let's leave now. Let's go."

Billy, the boy with the ice cream on his shirt, didn't care anymore.

He wasn't hurt. He looked at Karl and the size of his paws, the broad crown of his head, the bare spots on his back, and the scars that were still red. "This big, big dog. He ain't trouble at all. Mister Policeman, he's an awesome dog!" Before Bill said, "Bye," he bent over and kissed Karl's head. As a parade of people parted, the police officer looped a large lasso around Karl's collar and lugged him toward his patrol car.

Karl did not bark.

"No!" Jeff hurtled up the back steps of the stage. "No! Karl is my dog. He didn't mean to make these many mistakes. He hasn't been happy. He's been hungry and hurt. He needs me to walk him and teach him some rules. He thinks he's too big, but he's just right for me. He was found tied to a fence. I rescued him. He'll have a home with me and plenty of food, some toys and we'll take walks on the beach. The terrible truth—at times, we've all been lost and alone. We can teach each other about learning to love. Please, sir, please, may I take him home?"

The police officer told Jeff that his dog would need to learn not to run. Then he happily handed the rope to Jeff. "Time to take trouble home," he said, half serious and half smiling.

"Let's go home," said Jeff to Karl.

Karl looked up and his bright amber eyes mellowed as they seemed to say to Jeff, "Thanks for saving me."

Then suddenly, Karl leaped into the air and began to jump up and down, up and down, up and down, tail wagging wildly, huge hind end wiggling and waving. He lifted his broad head, and with riotous roar, he barked *ruff, ruff, ruff—* "Take me home."

Karl was happy now. He had a home and a hero. He learned to bark. Karl had found his voice, and a way to tell Jeff, "I love you. I will never run away again. "

And he never did.

The End

Jeff's Note

I have always loved dogs. My career in music and long road tours, did not allow me to have a dog. Oh sure, I tried. I was given a dog that I named Max after a dog I had as a kid. Circumstances were too difficult for Max and for me. I ended up looking to find a new safe home for him. I remember feeling a little ashamed and disappointed in myself. Still, I knew that what I did to Max was *for Max*. After that, it was never ending continual desire for a special companion, a forever canine pooch pal, my unconditional best friend. I hoped one day to have one big happy boy whom I loved and 'HE' to be me and 'ME' to be he. Looking back, I knew that sooner or later these prayers would become him.

As I traveled across Europe, I loved to take pictures and, usually, it was of dogs I met. I remember asking complete strangers to pose for pictures with their pets. When I snapped the shot, it was usually of just the dog and a set of knees and feet. My heart was engaged in capturing four legged pals with soft gentle eyes, ears any which way, and wildly encouraging wagging tails. My collection of photos seemed to grow and grow. For a brief time, it temporarily tapped over my desire to have a real furry guy of my own.

Prayers answered, many years later, my phone snapped alive with a picture of a large yellow lab that needed a home. Immediately, my thoughts posed myself in a picture with him. Karl became mine and I became his on this one May special day. Together we share a Doggie Dad's beachside bungalow. Long nights alone have become shorter, and I jump out of bed each morning to go for our walk just the "boy and me".

A big thanks and shout out to the many talented and amazing artist that have understood me and I to them, my family, and Karl's big heaping of love from Penny and Klydee who have become his second home when I am away on tour. And, thank you to all the pups and people that I have photo'd on my journeys doing 'this and that'. Yes, I am still taking pictures, and as you can guess, lots and lots of them are of my kid; silly, smilin' Karl. Just maybe, new prayers and prayers have been known to be answered, there will be a time with no more *aways* for me and with little or no time away from Karl. And, just maybe, again, my new gig will be taking photos of Karl rocking on and 'wiggle butting' joy and comfort to those in need and an engaging and remarkable rally of Rock n Roll musical, my long time, *magical* friends. Y'all be cool.

May God Bless You,
Jeff

Special Thanks

The authors, Penny Wagner and Jeff Ousley, lovingly acknowledge the amazing talents of rock guitar legend, voice extraordinaire, and Rock and Roll Hall of Fame member, Nancy Wilson. We sincerely wish to express to our readership the heartfelt gratitude we hold for Nancy. Her special narration of our audio book; Karl the Grateful Dog, is warmly acknowledged.

"Thank you, Nancy. May the enormity of the favor that you have shared with us be the good that we share with others. We pray that your gift of kindness, and the message of rescue, will multiply many, many times to everyone everywhere with returning joys back to you."

Love
from the Grateful Team,
Jeff and Penny and…Karl

Karl
the Grateful Dog

also available in
eBook version & audiobook

Karl's story is a lesson for us all. If we trust them,
they will trust and love us even more.
Help us spread this beautiful story. Give Karl some love!

You may leave a message/review in Amazon.com

support us
@karlthegratefuldog

ask Karl some questions
Karlthegratefuldog@gmail.com